Contents

How to use this book	4
The National Tests	6
Section 1: Writing non-fiction	8
Section 2: Writing fiction	18
Section 3: Reading comprehension	28
Section 4: Spelling	40
Section 5: Punctuation	44
Section 6: Vocabulary	50
Section 7: Reviewing your work	54
Section 8: Handwriting	55

The answers can be found in a pull-out section in the middle of this book.

How to use this book

Writing non-fiction (pages 8 to 17)

① Definition – This explains the topic simply and explains why it is important.

② Text plan – This section gives a step-by-step guide to help you plan your writing.

③ Guided writing – A piece of writing based on the text plan with additional assistance.

④ Independent writing – This gives further opportunities for writing long or short pieces of a similar style.

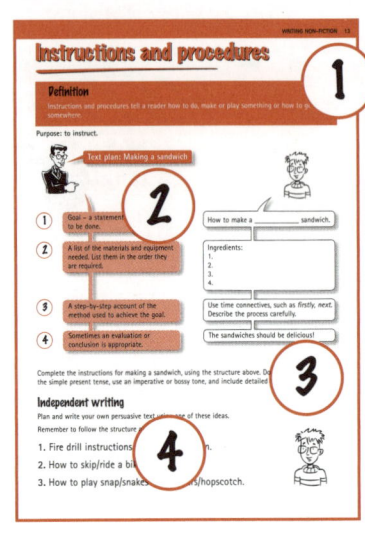

Writing fiction 1 (pages 18 to 23)

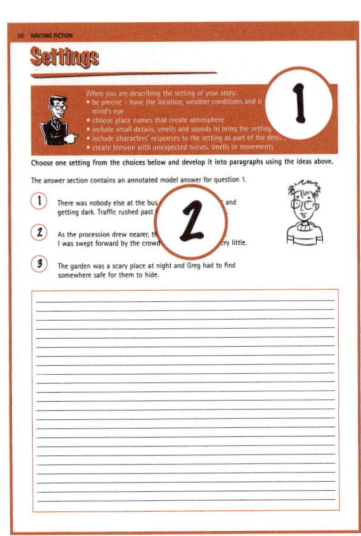

① Revision notes – Supportive notes that give brief guidance on the questions below.

② Activity choice – A range of three activities to complete as either a short (20 minutes) or long (45 minutes) piece of writing.

Writing fiction 2 (pages 24 to 27)

① Guided writing question – An exercise to be completed using the framework.

② Story scaffold – Provides structure and support, as well as space to plan your writing. Answers provide more detail on writing style and structure.

③ Independent writing – A range of three independent writing pieces that can be completed as part of a short or long task.

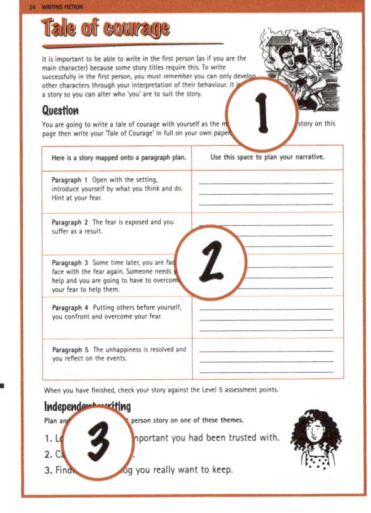

Reading comprehension (pages 28 to 39)

① The text – A range of texts are given, including fiction, non-fiction and poetry.

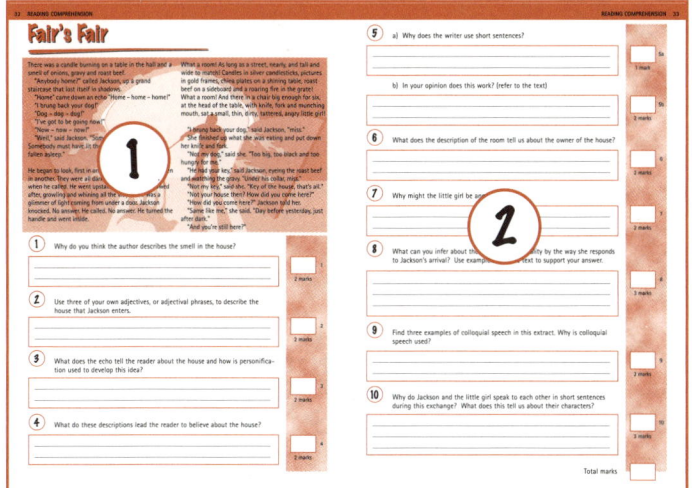

② The questions – Comprehension questions that allow you to demonstrate your Level 5 skills. Number of marks available and space to complete answers are given.

Additional support

Spelling practice (pages 40 to 43)

These exercises are designed to give useful practice in the more difficult areas of spelling – plurals, tenses and common errors.

Punctuation (pages 44 to 49)

A range of exercises covering key Level 5 punctuation, includes work on the use of ellipses, dashes and semi-colons. It also includes a quick punctuation test.

Vocabulary (pages 50 to 53)

The vocabulary exercises focus on improving your writing by making sure that 'every word counts'. Each section has a brief explanation followed by exercises in developing and using a Level 5 vocabulary.

Reviewing your work and Handwriting (pages 54 to 55)

Supportive notes and examples of how to review your writing continually (especially in tests) and handwriting styles that achieve Levels 3, 4 and 5.

The National Tests

Key Facts

- The Key Stage 2 National Tests (or SATs) take place in the middle of May in Year 6. You will be tested on Maths, English and Science.
- The tests take place in your school and will be marked by examiners – not your teacher!
- You will get your results in July, two months after you take the tests.
- Individual test scores are not made public but a school's combined scores are published in what are commonly known as league tables.

The English National Tests

You will take four tests in English. These are designed to test your Reading, Writing and Spelling. Your handwriting will be assessed through the Writing Tests.

Don't forget!

1) There is now one long and one short Writing Test (instead of two long ones).
2) There will be a new mark scheme for Writing.
3) Handwriting will be assessed in the Writing Test – there is no separate handwriting test.

The Writing Tests

There are now two Writing Tests – one short (about 20 minutes) and one longer test (about 45 minutes). Remember to keep your handwriting neat for these tests.

The Short Writing Task is 20 minutes long. You will have some time to plan and space on the paper to make brief notes but remember that you only have 20 minutes to write your piece.

The Long Writing Task is 45 minutes long. You will have about 10 minutes to plan and there should be some space to write notes too. Remember you only have 45 minutes to complete the whole task!

Where to go to get help
Pages 8 to 27 are designed to help you succeed in the Writing Tests and include a variety of long and short tasks.
Pages 44 to 54 will help you to give 'voice' to your writing, sharpen up your punctuation and improve your grammar.

The Reading Test

There is one test to assess your reading comprehension. It will last about 1 hour. In this test, you will be given a series of texts and an answer paper. You will be allowed to use the texts to answer the questions, so you won't need to memorise them.

Where to go to get help
Pages 28 to 39 give you practice in answering reading comprehension questions, which will help with the Reading Test.

The Spelling Test

There is one 15 minute Spelling Test. Your teacher will read a passage (or play a cassette with someone else reading the passage). You will have to write the words to complete the passage.

Where to go to get help
Pages 40 to 43 give you practice in spelling.

The Short Writing Task

Pages 20 to 23 give you an opportunity to practise elements of a complete narrative. You can use these activities to practise writing for 20 minutes. Set your clock and start writing!

Pages 12 to 17 allow you to practise writing non-fiction pieces. You can vary the time you use between 20 and 45 minutes to give you practice in each test.

Practising non-fiction text features

The passive voice or impersonal writing

Non-fiction writing often uses the passive voice – that is, the tone is impersonal, e.g. *The ingredients are mixed* rather than *First you mix the ingredients*. This tone is important because it gives an air of authority to the account you are writing, but it needs practice. It is very easy to slip into a more casual and personal tone.

Practise writing impersonally by working through these examples.
Re-write these sentences. Can you identify what text type is being used?

1 When you are making a cake you have to remember to heat up the oven first. Heat it up to about 190 °C and then, while you are mixing the ingredients, it is heating up nicely.

> *When you are baking a cake you have to remember to heat up the oven first. Heat it up to about 190°c and then, while you are mixing the ingredients it will heat up nicely.*

2 Lots of people think that smoking is bad for you and I agree. They think that it can damage your lungs and I have read research from doctors that confirms this view.

> *Lots of people think that smoking is bad for you and I agree. They think that it can damage your lungs and I have researched from ~~research~~ doctors that confirms this view.*

3 When you are playing snakes and ladders, you and the other players have to take it in turns to throw the dice. If you land on a square with a ladder on, it's good news and you go up. But if you land on a snake, you have to travel down the snake. Bad luck!

Informal and formal description

Non-fiction writing requires an impersonal, authoritative tone. Using the passive voice is important, and so is appropriate description. Do **not** use description that is

1) flowery and/or atmospheric – this is more appropriate for some types of fiction writing;
2) informal 'street talk' – use adjectives carefully.

Re-write these sentences using appropriate description.

1) School uniform can cast many a teenager into the depths of despair. It's unflattering, uncool and shabby. How can you look your best for school in these harsh, scratchy and dull materials?

_____
_____
_____

2) If you have ever walked down a dirty, litter-strewn street, with fast-food wrappings blowing about wistfully in the wind, you will understand and empathise with me over the problem of litter.

_____
_____
_____

3) Even picking up the fresh bread can get your tastebuds going when you're making a sandwich. Of course, getting soft, creamy butter and delicious, home-made jam is important too, for the best in home sandwich creation.

_____
_____
_____

4) Walking home alone one dark, gloomy and rainy night, Nadia was surprised to find herself surrounded by young, aggressive-looking men. It was obvious that they only wanted one thing – her mobile phone!

_____
_____
_____

Simple present tense

Apart from recounts (which are written in the past tense), non-fiction texts tend to be written in the simple present tense. That means you write as if something is happening at that time. This helps make your writing clear and easy for the reader to understand. It also shows that the information is still relevant – not in the past but still important to the reader today.

Put these sentences into the simple present tense.

1 Water has covered three-quarters of the Earth's surface for years, and most of this was held in the oceans.

2 Pollinated flowers have had their pollen taken from the male to the female part of the flower, so that fertilisation can happen and fruits and seeds can be made.

3 Migrating birds covered enormous distances. For example, the Arctic Tern flew across the world to the Antarctic.

4 Litter looked unsightly. It spoilt a beauty spot and made a run-down area look worse.

Connectives

Connectives are important in non-fiction text. They link different parts of the text together. They give the writing structure and organisation and so help to focus and clarify the reader's mind. This is particularly important as the reader will be trying to receive information from the piece of writing.

Connectives can be time (first, then, next, when), causal or logical (therefore, consequently, furthermore, because).

Use an appropriate connective to complete these sentences. Sometimes there might be more than one appropriate connective.

1. _____, put out the cake ingredients.

   _____, blend the butter and sugar.

2. _____, people say that watching television can be damaging. _____, opponents of this view argue that TV can be stimulating and enjoyable.

3. _____ the break in, two men were seen running down the road. _____, a police officer was just turning into the road in his car.

4. Water vapour cools down _____ clouds are formed. _____ it rains, when the cloud is so 'heavy' that the rain has to fall to the ground.

5. _____, smokers do use up many hospital beds because of smoking-related diseases.

   _____ these beds are not available to those who are seriously ill through no fault of their own.

Persuasion

Definition
A persuasive text tries to make the reader think, do or buy something.

Purpose: to persuade.

Text plan: Should everyone pick up litter?

1. Start with a clear presentation of the point to be argued, followed by a summary of the main arguments.

   Introduce the problem of litter. What/where is it? What are the options for tidying up?

2. Paragraphs should be presented in a logical order. Each paragraph should present a point supporting the argument with evidence and examples that strengthen the case.

   Arguments for picking up litter.
   1. Looks unsightly
   2. Wildlife damage
   3. Environmental impact
   4. Role of council and individuals

3. Reiteration – a summary of the arguments followed by a repetition of the opening assertion.

   Repeat the main points and assertion from beginning paragraph.

Write a piece of persuasive writing about litter, following the structure above. Don't forget to use connectives, and use the simple present tense.

Independent writing

Plan and write your own persuasive text using one of these ideas.

Remember to follow the structure above.

1. Cruelty to pets is outdated and needs to be stopped.
2. Smoking hurts everyone.
3. A balanced diet is good for you.
4. Some television is good for you.

Instructions and procedures

Definition
Instructions and procedures tell a reader how to do, make or play something or how to get somewhere.

Purpose: to instruct.

Text plan: Making a sandwich

1. Goal – a statement of what needs to be done.

2. A list of the materials and equipment needed. List them in the order they are required.

3. A step-by-step account of the method used to achieve the goal.

4. Sometimes an evaluation or conclusion is appropriate.

How to make a _____ sandwich.

Ingredients:
1.
2.
3.
4.

Use time connectives, such as *firstly*, *next*. Describe the process carefully.

The sandwiches should be delicious!

Complete the instructions for making a sandwich, using the structure above. Don't forget to write in the simple present tense, use an imperative or bossy tone, and include detailed factual information.

Independent writing

Plan and write your own persuasive text using one of these ideas.

Remember to follow the structure above.

1. Fire drill instructions for your classroom.

2. How to skip/ride a bike.

3. How to play snap/snakes and ladders/hopscotch.

Explanation

Definition
An explanation tells the reader how or why something works or happens. It can be about natural things, e.g. why volcanoes erupt, or about mechanical things, e.g. how a telephone works.

Purpose: to explain.

Text plan: Water and the water cycle

1. Start with a clear and precise definiton of the phenomenon. Use simple present tense.

   Water is essential. Describe its formation.

2. Describe the parts.

   Use this paragraph to describe how much water there is and where it exists.

3. Describe the operation in a step-by-step, logical way.

   Look at the water cycle in more detail. Use appropriate technical terms. Explain the cycle, possibly with a diagram.

4. Explain where and when it is used.

   Describe the main function of water in maintaining life and other aspects, such as water schemes for generating electricity.

5. You may need to add information about special features. Then finish with a summing up paragraph that completes the explanation.

   Water in three states of matter. Sum up – recycling.

Complete this explanation of the water cycle, making sure you use (and explain if necessary) the correct technical language. Use clear language and write in the simple present tense.

Independent writing

Plan and write your own explanation using one of these ideas.
Remember to use the structure above.

1. How the digestive system works.

2. How do plants get pollinated?

3. What happens when a kettle is boiled?

WRITING NON-FICTION 15

Non-chronological report

Definition

Non-chronological reports give a reader information about something or somewhere. They are usually about a group of things, e.g. dinosaurs, not one thing in particular, e.g. Dilly the dinosaur. Facts about the subject are organised into paragraphs.

Purpose: to give information.

Text plan: Migration

1. Introduce the topic with a definition and follow this up with more technical classification. Make it clear what the report will be about.

   What is migration? Which animals does it affect?

2. Give a description of the subject by some of its qualities or uses.

   Migration for warmth – give examples. Use time connectives, such as *firstly*, *next*. Describe the process carefully.

3. Follow with a number of paragraphs, each one presenting detailed information on a different aspect of the topic.

   Look at different aspects of migration, such as distance covered, routes used, the different kinds of animals that migrate.

4. Return to some of the main points as an ending comment.

   Mystery and wonder of migration.

Complete this non-chronological report about migration. You will need to find extra information from suitable non-fiction texts, such as an encyclopedia. Make sure you keep your writing descriptive but not imaginative. Do not give opinions, but use good clear examples.

Independent writing

Plan and write your own non-chronological report using one of these ideas.

Remember to use the structure above.
You will need to gather information from appropriate non-fiction sources.

1. Mountains

2. The monarchy in Great Britain

3. The Earth and the Solar System

Balanced argument

Definition
A balanced argument gives the reader information about an issue from different points of view, then leaves the reader to make up their mind about how they feel about the issue.

Purpose: to present a balanced argument.

Text plan: Should school uniform be compulsory?

1. Start with a statement of the ISSUE under discussion and an overview of the main arguments.

   Introduce the issue and outline the main approaches taken by schools over school uniform.

2. State the arguments FOR and give evidence to back them up. This could be more than one paragraph.

   Cover the main points.
   1. Neat and functional
   2. Inexpensive
   3. Sense of identity

3. State the arguments AGAINST and give evidence to back them up. This could be more than one paragraph.

   Cover the main points.
   1. Unattractive
   2. Rules/time-wasting
   3. Lack of appreciation for individuals

4. End with your conclusion, based on a weighing up of the evidence.

   Decide on your conclusion, making sure it is based on the evidence.

Complete this balanced argument about school uniform, taking care to present both sides of the argument in an impersonal way. The conclusion should be personal, based on the evidence. Use the paragraph prompts above to organise your work.

Independent writing

Plan and write your own explanation using one of these ideas. Remember to use the structure above.

1. Should every child learn French at primary school?

2. Should every child take responsibility for some area of housework?

3. Should pocket money be compulsory?

Recount

Definition
A recount tells the reader about something that has happened in the past. It might have happened to the writer or to someone else.

Purpose: to retell an event or events.

Text plan: Newspaper report on street muggings

1. Orientation – this is the information that helps the reader understand the recount (who, where, when, why).

   Introduce the subject of mugging and the person to be interviewed about their experience.

2. Recount events in chronological order (as they happened), making sure the event is broken down clearly.

   Describe the interviewee in more detail. Why was he/she walking home late? Describe the events in a blow-by-blow way.

3. Give some personal comment or reflection about the event.

   Reflections about what else he/she could have done to keep safe.

4. Sum up by returning to some of the main points as an ending comment. Some evaluation may be appropriate.

   Evaluate on the impact on his/her life. Suggest action that might be taken.

Complete this recount about muggings in the form of a newspaper report, taking care to write chronologically and to use relevant detail and description. Make sure you use reported speech as part of your piece. Use the paragraph prompts to help you shape your answer.

Independent writing

Plan and write your own recount using one of these ideas.
Remember to use the structure above.

1. The diary entry of Henry VIII after he had decided to execute Anne Boleyn.
2. A letter to an aunt from someone who met the Queen at a Jubilee celebration.
3. A biography of your life so far.

Narrative writing

This is a basic format of a narrative.

Beginning	Build up	Climax	Resolution	Reflection
when the characters and setting are introduced	a series of events leading up to the point of the story	the problem, or event, happens	a sorting out or fixing of the problem	by major characters or author on the events

 A Level 5 story will include the following features:
- description
- action
- dialogue
- character reflections
- perhaps a narrator's comment

Once you have planned the narrative outline, plot these writers' techniques onto your paragraph plan to ensure a balanced story.

2 Before you start you must decide whether you will write in the **first person** (I, me, we) or the **third person** (he, she, they).

First person	Third person
Diaries, letters, autobiographies, retelling a personal experience and writing as a specific character must be in the first person.	Many stories are written in the third person. These are generally easier to write. As narrator you know what all the characters are doing and thinking. You can skip between locations in the tale.

Once you have decided which person to write in, make sure you stick with it!

 You must hook your reader from the start so plan the opening sentence with care. You could choose:
- Dialogue – *"Ow ow ow," screamed Baby Bear as he spat out the porridge. "This is too hot to eat!"*
- Action – *Slamming the front door behind them, the three bears strode off into the forest.*
- Setting – *Early one spring morning, as the forest creatures scuttled busily about their business, three bears set off for a walk.*
- Character – *Goldilocks was a rather spoilt and very stubborn child.*
- Traditional – *Once upon a time, in the heart of a great forest, there lived three bears.*

 Plan the ending. This is really important as a weak ending will ruin a good story.
- Contrast with the beginning – a frail and lonely old man from the introduction could be rosy-cheeked and smiling contentedly in the final paragraph.
- Character could reflect – *One thing is for certain, never again will I . . .*
- Hint at the future – *"Every last drop", those were dad's words, "get rid of every last drop". But if I get rid of every last drop of potion then I'll never visit Bhalstron again.*
- Characters discuss the events – *"Do you think they are going to believe us?" Lucas asked as they rang the bell. "Well, we'll soon find out," Rani muttered.*

WRITING FICTION 19

Use this page for your writer's notes and jottings of words, phrases and ideas that you can use in future story writing. Some examples have been given for you.

Character
- a smile playing around her lips
- tapping impatiently with her fingernails on the wooden chair arms
- I may be old-fashioned but …

Settings
- dawn was creeping over the horizon
- the chink in the curtains the only source of light
- the gentle hum of distant traffic

Flashback sentence starters
- Was it really only yesterday that …
- She remembered the first time they met …
- If only he could turn back the clock …

Descriptive time connectives
Level 5 writers say more than *first* or *next* and *later*.
- As the moon rose over the rooftops …
- Almost before they realised it …
- At that precise moment …

Tip
NEVER have more than two or three important characters; you will not have time to develop them realistically. Don't waste words on minor characters – *His friends jeered menacingly* will do for the bully's friends.

Settings

When you are describing the setting of your story:
- be precise - have the location, weather conditions and time of day in your mind's eye
- choose place names that create atmosphere
- include small details, smells and sounds to bring the setting alive
- include characters' responses to the setting as part of the description
- create tension with unexpected noises, smells or movements

Choose one setting from the choices below and develop it into paragraphs using the ideas above.

The answer section contains an annotated model answer for question 1.

1 There was nobody else at the bus stop. It was cold, wet and getting dark. Traffic rushed past but the bus didn't come.

2 As the procession drew nearer, the cheering grew louder. I was swept forward by the crowd but could still see very little.

3 The garden was a scary place at night and Greg had to find somewhere safe for them to hide.

Character descriptions

When writing about your characters, you do not need too much description – just those details that make the character special, things you'd notice on first meeting them. Develop your character through what they think, say and do, and by contrasting them with others. Avoid telling how a character feels; rather, show it in their behaviour.

Choose one character from the choices below and develop it into paragraphs using the ideas above. Include the use of speech to show character.

The answer section contains an annotated model answer for question 1.

1. A new child in the class, prim, neat appearance, and very self-assured described by the main character in the story.

2. Introduce the main character, a proud and determined boy who is being unfairly accused of cheating in a test. He gives no explanation because that would implicate another child.

3. A child coming home to an angry parent. He/she left their bedroom in a frightful mess.

Dialogue

- Use dialogue to develop your character in a way that is relevant to the plot.
- Use it instead of action to move the story along (but take care not to overuse it). Dialogue is not simply speech, it is also **how** characters speak.
- Vary the way you report speech. You must use adverbs and strong verbs but too many sounds contrived; a simple 'he said' could be the best choice.
- Always make it obvious who is speaking. You must use correct speech punctuation.

Choose one scene from the choices below and use dialogue to develop it into paragraphs using the ideas above.

The answer section contains an annotated model answer for question 1.

① An unexpected caller talking through a letterbox to a child who has been told not to open the door to anyone.

② Two children find an unusual package.

③ A woman in a shop has her purse stolen. A teenage girl chases after the suspect.

Characters' reflections and narrators' comments

- Develop depth in characters by showing inner conflicts through their reflections; these thoughts should be connected with *but* or *on the other hand*.
- Characters can reflect on changes within themselves - a good way to end a story.
- Contrast two characters, or develop their relationship, by showing the reflections of both on the same event.
- Narrator's comments are a way of including another viewpoint, summarising events or influencing the reader's view of characters.

Choose one scene from the choices below and use reflections and the narrator's comments to develop it into paragraphs using the ideas above.

The answer section contains an annotated model answer for question 1.

① A girl is given a present by her grandmother. She is sure it will be an unwanted knitted cardigan. Mother is watching, scared that her daughter will be rude about the gift.

② Tom found a fox cub and tried to keep it but eventually realised that it was unkind to make it into a pet. He is in the kitchen with his dad, having just returned from the animal refuge where they left the cub. It is the end of the story.

③ At a sleepover, one child hears a strange noise and wants to go to investigate. The other child is tired and doesn't want to get out of bed.

_____
_____
_____
_____
_____
_____
_____
_____
_____
_____
_____
_____
_____
_____
_____
_____
_____

Tale of courage

It is important to be able to write in the first person (as if you are the main character) because some story titles require this. To write successfully in the first person, you must remember you can only develop other characters through your interpretation of their behaviour. It is still a story so you can alter who 'you' are to suit the story.

Question

You are going to write a tale of courage with yourself as the main character. Plan your story on this page then write your 'Tale of Courage' in full on your own paper.

Here is a story mapped onto a paragraph plan.	Use this space to plan your narrative.
Paragraph 1 Open with the setting, introduce yourself by what you think and do. Hint at your fear.	
Paragraph 2 The fear is exposed and you suffer as a result.	
Paragraph 3 Some time later, you are face to face with the fear again. Someone needs your help and you are going to have to overcome your fear to help them.	
Paragraph 4 Putting others before yourself, you confront and overcome your fear.	
Paragraph 5 The unhappiness is resolved and you reflect on the events.	

When you have finished, check your story against the Level 5 assessment points.

Independent writing

Plan and write another first person story on one of these themes.

1. Losing something important you had been trusted with.
2. Caught telling a lie.
3. Finding a stray dog you really want to keep.

Tales of long ago

To achieve Level 5, you must show understanding of the features and style of a traditional tale. Good-versus-evil characterisation is the most important feature. You must conclude with a resolution (tying up) of the story FOLLOWED by reflections, showing the impact of the events on some key characters, and END WITH a moral and/or 'happily ever after'.

Question

You are going to write a traditional story with the youngest child of three as the hero and a seemingly insignificant gift saving him/her. Plan your story on this page then write your 'Tale of Long Ago' in full on your own paper.

Here is a story mapped onto a paragraph plan.	Use this space to plan your narrative.
Paragraph 1 Traditional tale opening. Introduce the hero (good), the youngest of three brothers/sisters (cowardly, selfish etc.).	
Paragraph 2 Characters required to do a good deed; first two fail/refuse.	
Paragraph 3 Youngest needs to do his/her own deed; involves a sacrifice; makes the right choice and is rewarded with a gift or advice.	
Paragraph 4 Some time later the hero faces an improbable challenge. The 'gift' comes to his aid and he succeeds.	
Paragraph 5 The hero's improved circumstances explained and 'bad' characters reform or are punished. The moral and 'happily ever after'.	

When you have finished, check your story against the Level 5 assessment points.

Independent writing

Plan and write your own traditional tale around one of these themes.

1. Three wishes – the first two are wasted.
2. A young man sets out to make his fortune.
3. Good deeds leading to the release of someone trapped in an ugly/unpleasant form.

A cautionary tale

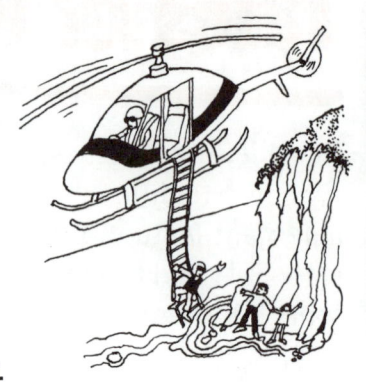

To achieve Level 5, it is necessary to vary the straightforward timeline of events. One technique for doing this is using a flashback.

Question

You are going to write a cliff rescue story following a flashback structure. Plan on this page then write your 'Cautionary Tale' in full on your own paper.

Here is a story mapped onto a paragraph plan.	Use this space to plan your narrative.
Paragraph 1 The children are in trouble.	
Paragraph 2 FLASHBACK The parents' warning to the children earlier that day.	
Paragraph 3 The danger/trouble worsens.	
Paragraph 4 The rescue.	
Paragraph 5 Parents find out and their responses. Characters' reflection on the experience and lesson learned.	

When you have finished, check your story against the Level 5 assessment points.

Independent writing

Plan and write your own adventure or suspense story using one of these titles.

1. A Foolish Boast
2. Noises in the Night
3. Just Another Shopping Trip
4. The Unusual Gift

Start your story at an action point and use a flashback to fill in the events up to this point.

A historical tale

When writing historical stories, your planning must contain a few historical details that you will 'drop into the setting'. Be sure to plan an ending that goes beyond the 'happily ever after'. To achieve Level 5, you need to reflect back on events in your ending, as well as tying up loose ends.

Question

Your story will be set in Victorian times, with the main character trying to scrape together a living in the streets of London. Start this story with dialogue. Plan your story on this page then write your 'Historical Tale' in full on your own paper.

Here is a story mapped onto a paragraph plan.	Use this space to plan your narrative.
Paragraph 1 Start with the main character speaking, perhaps to themselves; continue with description to further introduce character and setting.	
Paragraph 2 Develop the character by contrasting with others. He/she sees a rich person drop something of value.	
Paragraph 3 Character considers whether or not to keep the item. Someone else affects the decision.	
Paragraph 4 He/she decides to give it back – the honest choice – and is rewarded generously.	
Paragraph 5 Describe the character in his/her improved circumstances. Have them reflect on their earlier poverty and show appreciation of their new situation.	

When you have finished, check your story against the Level 5 assessment points.

Independent writing

Plan and write a historical story set in one of the following.

1. Robin Hood's time
2. The Second World War
3. The Plague

Make the main character show honesty or generosity and be rewarded.

Reading comprehension

To achieve Level 5, you must understand and practise the four skills explained in the table below. The 2 and 3 mark questions always ask you to do one of these.

You must be able to...	Show it like this...
Deduce – draw conclusions from your reading	Draw out extra information from your reading – facts that are there but not actually told to you. Remember deductions change as a narrative develops.
Infer – go beyond what is in the text to draw conclusions based on your life experiences	Make predictions based on the book and your knowledge of how characters may respond. Use phrases like: *she probably* or *because people usually*.
Evaluate – decide how effective the writing is and comment on your personal response to it	Comment on the author's vocabulary choices and arrangement of sentences, and the use of techniques, such as withholding information from the reader. Say whether this successfully creates suspense, persuades you etc.
Justify – use parts of the text to back up what you are saying	Quote words and phrases in the text to support your answers in the other four areas.

For more support see **Achieve Level 5 English Revision**, page 38.

ENGLISH
Answers for Practice Questions

Answers

Page 8
The passive voice or impersonal writing
1. It is important to pre-heat the oven when making a cake. The oven should be turned on before mixing starts, so that it has plenty of time to reach 190 °C. (Instructions)
2. Many people think that smoking is dangerous and damaging to the smoker and others around the smoker. Recent research from doctors confirms a widely held belief that smoking can damage the lungs and have a negative effect on other parts of the body too. (Persuasion)
3. During snakes and ladders, the players take it in turns to throw the dice. When a player lands on a ladder, they can travel up the ladder. However, when a player lands on a snake, they have to travel down the snake. (Explanation)

Page 9
Informal and formal description
1. School uniform is a cause of gloom and despair for many young people who consider it most unattractive and unflattering. Their opinion of school uniform is shaped not only by the style but also by the material used, which is often scratchy and in dull colours.
2. Anyone walking along a city street would be able to describe the horrors of litter. Such problems are more obvious in bad weather, as wind can blow rubbish around making it even more noticeable.
3. Use fresh bread when making a sandwich, as it smells and tastes so much better than older, slightly stale bread. It is also advisable to use soft butter and home-made jam – the better the ingredients, the better the sandwich.
4. As Nadia walked home one wet, dark evening, she was startled to find herself surrounded by a group of aggressive-looking youths. They clearly wanted her mobile phone.

Page 10
Simple present tense
1. Water covers three-quarters of the Earth's surface – most of this is held in the oceans.
2. Pollinated flowers have their pollen taken from the male to the female part of the flower, so that fertilisation happens and fruits and seeds are made.
3. Migrating birds cover enormous distances. For example, the Arctic Tern flies across the world to the Antarctic.
4. Litter looks unsightly. It spoils a beauty spot and can make a run-down area look worse.

Page 11
Connectives
1. First/Firstly ... second/secondly/next/then/after that
2. On one hand...but/however/on the other hand
3. After...however/meanwhile/at that moment/at that instant/at that time
4. then/and ... So/As a result/
5. Meanwhile/Therefore...As a result /So/Meanwhile

Page 20
Settings
The yellow-grey storm clouds merged with the darkening sky as night crept in. Approaching headlights picked out patches of brilliance on the wet road and then streaked past, sending a fierce spray of icy water biting into her bare legs. Nobody else had ventured out on that desolate evening. Putting thoughts of cosy kitchens and warm feet out of her mind, she peered into the distance – was that a bus approaching? The oil tanker roared past and the road returned to darkness and silence.

A Level 5 answer should contain the following features.
- A detail – headlight on wet road.
- Using all senses – roaring oil tanker and silence, the water biting her legs.
- Making the reader use their imagination – look how the writer has said the character is alone and that she is waiting for a bus.
- The setting and character's behaviour are linked – detail is limited to what is necessary to the story line.
- Describing through the character's responses – adding to the development of the girl's character.
- A variety of sentence types is used to create an appropriate effect; metaphor and personification are used.

Page 21
Character descriptions
The first time I saw Eloise de Ferne she was standing beside Ms Headley, her hands primly clasped in front of her, a perfect black plait over one shoulder and an almost-smile flickering around her lips. Slowly her sharp eyes scanned the room. The class waited expectantly for her reply to the 'tell us about yourself, my dear' opening from Ms Headley. Her pause felt uncomfortably long. When she spoke, it was in a firm and clear voice.
  "It's difficult to know where to begin. It might be easier if you were to ask me some questions."
  Ms Headley's discomfort was all the more obvious beside Eloise's absolute confidence. Everyone sat up that bit taller as a this-could-become-interesting murmur ran around the room.

A Level 5 answer should contain the following features.
- Details of appearance are kept to those points that make the character special.
- The character is developed through her actions – her self-assurance is shown rather than stated.
- Contrasting with other characters – the teacher's discomposure serves to illustrate the extremes of Eloise's behaviour.
- Speech is used to show more of the character – let the reader decide on the character by hearing what they say.
- The character's feelings are shown rather than told.
- Including the reactions of others to the character– the narrative is moved on and questions are raised for the reader.

Page 22

Dialogue

The letterbox opened and Tyrone shivered as two dark eyes peered in.

"I know you're there, lad. I saw you through the front room window," a voice called softly. "Open the door a second, there's a good boy. I've got a parcel for your Mum."

"Leave it on the doorstep," Tyrone shouted back.

"Can't do that sonny," the voice said. "It's got to be signed for. Open up, there's a good boy."

Tyrone pressed himself into the corner of the hall where the eyes could not see him. Trying to sound much braver than he was feeling, he yelled, "No! I'm not allowed to. Go away!"

"You're not scared of me are you?" the voice cajoled.

"No! Go away!"

"No need to be scared son, I'm not going to hurt you. I just want to deliver this parcel." The voice was strained and sounding less friendly now. "Your Mum might be cross if she doesn't get it."

It was then that Tyrone had his flash of brilliance.

"OK," he replied sweetly. "I'll just run upstairs and wake her up." As he dashed up to his mother's empty bedroom, he heard the snap of the letterbox closing and crunch of footsteps on the gravel path. Only then did he permit himself a look out of the window.

A Level 5 answer should contain the following features.
- Variety in the way speech is reported – some use of adverbs (softly, sweetly), some strong speech verbs (cajoled, yelled) and some use of 'said'.
- Dialogue that moves the narrative along – this dialogue deals with a caller becoming increasingly intimidating and leads to the boy's trick, which exposes the caller as a 'baddie'.
- Develop characters – the voice at the door becomes more sinister as the writing develops.
- Make it obvious who is speaking – only once in the passage is the speaker not identified, and there it is obvious who is speaking, so a speech verb would have sounded clumsy.
- Correct speech punctuation.
- If the sentence ends when the speech ends, the full stop goes inside the closing speech marks.
- If the sentence continues after the speech, a comma goes inside the closing speech marks.
- Question marks and exclamation marks go inside the closing speech marks.
- A new paragraph is started for each new speaker in a passage of dialogue.

Page 23

Characters' reflections and narrators' comments

With mumbled thanks and an unenthusiastic smile, Sabrina began to remove the shiny wrapping paper. Why did everyone have to watch so closely? Sabrina didn't want to hurt her grandmother's feelings but she was being careful not to appear too grateful. She was determined to discourage Gran from knitting more disgusting pink fluffy cardigans. She imagined herself saying – why didn't you just give me the money the wool costs and let me buy something I'm actually going to wear – but knew she wouldn't.

Sabrina's mum, standing in the doorway, willed her daughter to be polite and not make a scene. She felt some sympathy for the girl, knowing only too well the disappointment of unwanted gifts, but there was no excuse for bad manners. Neither of them was aware that the old lady was sitting with her fingers crossed behind her back. An old lady who – like grandmothers the world over – just loved to make their grandchildren smile.

A Level 5 answer should contain the following features.
- The character's reflections add to the reader's understanding of their personality – e.g. Mum is someone who thinks feelings shouldn't get in the way of good manners.
- The dilemma creates a tension that draws the reader in – two conflicting courses of action are possible. Which will she take?
- Show events from more than one point of view – the relationship between Sabrina and her mum is developed through their thoughts.
- The author's comment is designed to influence the reader – making the grandmother good-intentioned and strengthening this viewpoint by likening her to most grandmothers.

Page 24

Tale of courage

Paragraph 1 In a first person narrative the setting will be described as seen by 'you'. Include the small details a child would notice – a fly on the window pane, the girl in front flicking paper. Put out some hooks for the reader by dropping hints of what is to come.

Paragraph 2 You should write about yourself in relation to others and track the effect the unfolding events have on you. The initial terror followed by the shame of being found out. This needs very powerful writing and would be a good place to use metaphor. Writing about what you imagine others to be thinking is another way to show the effect they are having on you. Include some dialogue to move the story on. Show the cruelty of others by their words and actions. Adjectives such as 'mocking' and 'scornful' could be used to describe the words and laughter. The imagined thoughts of others powerfully describe the effect of exposure on you.

Paragraph 3 Use a descriptive time connective to open the paragraph, e.g. 'Four long and lonely weeks later'. Develop your character by writing about the dilemma you face: doing what is right against doing what is comfortable. Enhance the description with physical aspects of fear (dry mouth, sweating palms). End with a cliffhanger.

Paragraph 4 This is an action paragraph and should be quite a contrast with the previous build up. Use short sentences and powerful verbs. Repetition may be a useful technique here – 'Ignoring the blood pounding in my ears, ignoring the nausea washing over me, ignoring my body screaming at me to stop, I strode forward'. End the paragraph with relief and amazement.

Paragraph 5 People's admiration could be described to resolve your unhappiness. Follow this with personal reflections. You need to show how you have been altered by the events. It could be that you feel much stronger now. Reflect on the fact that you will never again have to worry about your fear being exposed.

Page 25
Tales of long ago

Paragraph 1 Orientate the reader to a traditional tale by starting with a complex sentence. During the first paragraph, setting and characters are introduced. The storyline will be familiar so grip your readers with powerful and unusual descriptions.

Paragraph 2 In this paragraph you should develop the bad characters by their responses to the challenge and show the hero being selfless, good-natured, generous etc. at their failures (think of Cinderella). Writing about the older brothers/sisters, one at a time, you build anticipation of how the unlikely-sounding youngest will succeed where they have failed. The language, even dialogue, should be quite formal. Do not use contracted words such as couldn't or he'll.

Paragraph 3 To develop a more interesting main character show their inner reflections. These could be overcoming fear of danger or regrets at what must be given up to accept the challenge. End these musings with a firm decision to do the right thing. Characters could develop by how others, such as pets or a faithful servant, respond to them. The main character can also be seen as good for treasuring the 'gift', although it seems of little value. Success at this challenge is not the main event in the story, it is part of the build up to climax, so it must be kept snappy.

Paragraph 4 Move the story on in time with an interesting time connective. This paragraph is where you can use the 'gift' to help the hero achieve incredible things and triumph over the bad characters. Don't forget to vary the sentence types – short sentences for impact and use metaphor or simile to enhance your description.

Paragraph 5 Describe the main character in their new state of happiness. The natural environment often mirrors this – the sun shines, flowers bloom, birds sing and if you want rain this should gently caress the hero. The bad characters usually suffer remorse or envy and that is their punishment but never quite stop being bad. They are often forgiven by the hero who lives happily ever after.

Page 26
A cautionary tale

Paragraph 1 This story starts with a crisis and must have a powerful first sentence. Effective action writing depends on the use of some short punchy sentences, powerful verbs and questions to make the reader wonder. Tension is created using techniques such as repetition or alliteration. This paragraph should develop the setting and begin to build up characters by their responses to the crisis.

Paragraph 2 This should be more than a retelling of previous events. It is a chance to develop the character through their reflection and feelings. Vary the sentence types you use. Plant a sentence that you are going to refer back to in your concluding remarks.

Paragraph 3 Use dialogue to develop characters and move the story forward. Show the relationship between characters by how they speak to each other and develop more than one viewpoint. Include information from all senses as the setting is described.

Paragraph 4 Use a descriptive time connective to move the story on to the rescue. You must create some tension when the success of the operation is in the balance – ellipsis would help create this. Do not aim to tell it all; leave the tale when help is arriving. Use powerful language – strong verbs, metaphors, short sentences for impact followed by longer ones to give more information.

Paragraph 5 Use another time connective phrase to move the story to safety, the consequences and reflections. Show how the experience has changed your character. End with a narrator's comment that ties in with an earlier part of the story.

Page 27
A historical tale

Paragraph 1 You should use the first paragraph to establish your main character in the midst of Victorian London street life. Give your setting a name – any London landmark will do. Use the setting to say something about your character. Include sense impressions to develop the setting – what can the character see and hear? Add historical details as you describe incidents.

Paragraph 2 Use this paragraph to build up sympathy for the character through how others treat him/her, ignoring him/her, laughing etc. Develop tension with questions. Use simile or metaphor to describe the hunger. To keep the reader interested you should end this paragraph with a snappy suspense sentence – something is about to happen, but what will it be?

Paragraph 3 Use the main character's thoughts and reflections to explore the dilemma they are facing. Use language from a balanced argument to describe these – 'but there again', 'on the other hand'. Don't neglect sense impressions: the feel of the object, cold, hunger. For variety and interest, it is a good idea to introduce another character in this paragraph – good or bad – whose actions will influence the decision. This character does not need to know the effect they are having, in fact a secret between the main character and reader is what makes for Level 5 writing. Keep your reader guessing by ending this paragraph with the decision made but not shared with the reader.

Paragraph 4 A descriptive time connective will move your character to the point of returning the object. It would be a good idea to use dialogue here.

Paragraph 5 Tie up the loose ends by a couple of sentences about what happened since receiving the reward. Your character should reflect on events and make some observations on what they've learned about human nature or honesty. You could show their generosity by having them decide to use their good fortune to help others.

ANSWERS

Page 30
Chicken Dinner

1   Acceptable answers would be:
    - They've known her since she was first hatched.
    - She had escaped being killed by the mongoose.
    - She had been promised to the children as a pet.
    Use your knowledge of how children usually respond to pets to answer the second part.
    2 marks

2   You must refer to the Caribbean dialect used and the fact that chickens are kept by the family.
    2 marks

3   You have to look carefully and use your knowledge of chickens to find this answer. She has not yet started to lay eggs and so is probably a young hen. She is referred to as a chicken so is older than a chick and chicks wouldn't have enough meat on to be worth eating. The child says 'She not even had a chance fe lay yet' to argue that it is not fair to kill her when she is so young.
    2 marks

4   This question is about the feelings the poet evokes through her choice of words. It is also about identifying and empathising with Mama.
    Acceptable answers would be:
    - By giving Henrietta a name she becomes an individual to Mama.
    - Mama changes her mind after the name is used because she is also fond of the chicken.
    - Mama is reminded by the name that it is her child's pet and she doesn't want to upset her child.
    2 marks

5   This question is asking you to plot the changes in mood as they develop. It is also asking you to make deductions about the writer's emotions. You must mention the child's realisation that all the reasons why Henrietta should not be killed could be applied to all other hens. They are beginning to generalise. You MUST refer to the text.
    Up to 3 marks

Page 32
Fair's Fair

1   Acceptable answers would be:
    - To suggest that someone is living there.
    - To give the impression that the house (and the owner) are friendly and welcoming.
    You must make 2 points to get 2 marks

2   Answers must reflect the facts, i.e. lots of empty rooms leads to echoing. This question does not ask for your impression, so words such as frightening are not appropriate. Your choices may include: echoing, shadowy, deserted, welcoming smells, empty, unoccupied, grand.
    2 marks will be awarded for more adventurous word choices

3   The echo tells us the house is large and possibly deserted. Personification – 'a staircase that lost itself in shadows' – is used to say that the staircase is so enormous a candle is not sufficient to light it all.
    Answer both sections for 2 marks

4   The descriptions build up the feeling that someone/something mysterious is waiting in the house. They build tension towards something happening and lead to feelings of expectation.
    2 marks if the answer contains more than one point

5   a) Short sentences create tension and have a strong impact on the reader.
    b) Short sentences act in contrast to the surrounding longer sentences and keep the reader's interest. Repetition of a short sentence keeps the issue alive and tells the reader what to focus on. Short sentences in the dialogue reflect the children's lack of conversational skills and that they 'speak the same language' (dialect).
    1 mark for the impact of short sentences. You need to develop the first part of your answer and refer to the text for the other 2 marks

6   Acceptable answers would be: rich, tasteful, generous, likes art/ornaments, ostentatious. You should mention two of these and refer to the part of the text you are basing your deductions on.
    2 marks for 2 descriptive words and text references

7   Acceptable answers would be:
    - He has come in to spoil her peace.
    - She doesn't like dogs/boys.
    - He reminds her of being poor and hungry and she wants to forget all of that.
    - She has had a hard life and doesn't know what the future holds.
    Any 2 of these would get you 2 marks

8   Acceptable answers would be:
    - Self assured, confident, unhurried – she finishes her mouthful before speaking.
    - Brave – she shows no fear to an unknown boy and a dog.
    - Used to looking after herself – she has a key to the house.
    Up to 3 marks for 2 characteristics and justifying the answer from the text

9   The three examples of colloquial speech are:
    "I brung back your dog!" "I've got to be going now!" "Same like me."
    It has been used to show they are both poor children without education.
    2 marks for all 3 examples and a reason

10 Acceptable answers would be:
    - They are checking each other out.
    - Gathering information about each other.
    - They speak the same type of English.
    - They realise they are on the same level, straightforward, etc.
    Up to 3 marks. Most marks will be given for answers that deal with their characters and their position in Victorian society

Page 34

Applemoon

1. The simile is describing the house as settled, comfortable, contented, peaceful. The poet is alert, wakeful, could even be woken by moonlight.

   2 contrasting adjectives to describe the poet and the house will get you 2 marks

2. Acceptable answers would be:
   - clouds going quickly across the sky
   - bright moonlight flooding the garden
   - a lot of apples lying under spiky silver trees
   - trees in the moonlight

   NB Sea-stones is incorrect. She cannot see them – the description is a simile

   To get 2 marks you must mention at least 2 things

3. a) Examples are 'singing soft', 'ripe reluctant', 'close and curious', 'curling in the cold'.
   b) Your interpretations of why these are used could be:
   - To make the reader look at the description again/closely.
   - To cluster the description/make it more powerful.
   - Create a balance within the verse.

   1 mark for the alliterations. To get the full 3 marks the answer must deal with the poet's intentions

4. The shadow detached from the poet and stayed in the garden after the poet went back upstairs. Your interpretations of why could be:
   - To experience the moonlight.
   - To echo the apple picking.
   - To show the poet doesn't really want to go back indoors.

   To get the full 3 marks the answer must mention both what is described and the feelings it suggests

5. Words linked with a hyphen are: startle-sound, moon-flood, mouse-went, sea-stone, quick-ran, sleepy-warm. Your interpretations of why these are used could be:
   - Because it's unexpected and therefore effective.
   - To make the reader look at the description again.
   - To add rhythm/atmosphere to the poem.
   - To create contrast within longer sentences.

   1 mark for the hyphenated words. For the other 2 marks you must give a well reasoned answer covering at least 2 points

6. Both yes and no are acceptable answers but either must be supported with reasons. Your reasons could include the power of the description, whether you think the poet successfully evokes mood or whether the poet hooks the reader's interest. All of these must be supported with text references.

   For 2 marks you must support your opinion with at least 2 reasons

Page 36

Fire, Bed and Bone

1. The narrator is a dog. Evidence for this could be: her talk of knowing fireside and bone, describing herself as 'no hand-fed house dog', carrying a pup in her mouth, being patted and licking Comfort's hand.

   1 mark for dog and 2 marks for 2 supporting points

2. He lit a fire, died a long time ago and was wearing armour when he died.

   2 marks for all 3 points

3. You MUST give reasons from the evidence for your ideas. Acceptable answers could be:
   - He was hiding from great danger. He was armed and died in there rather than come out and face it.
   - He was being chased by enemy soldiers and had found a good hiding place. He was wearing armour and had built a fire, so obviously he had decided to remain there for a while.

   2 marks for 2 pieces of evidence to support your idea

4. Fleabane is a puppy. He is very young because he is carried in the narrator's mouth and is too young to hunt or eat rabbit. His mother feeds him and he sleeps a lot.

   1 mark for puppy and 2 marks for 2 supporting points

5. The relationship is between dog and owners. The narrator obviously loves Rufus and Comfort so adjectives could be: affectionate, devoted, loyal, kind, loving.

   3 marks

6. They are locked up in a stable, kept prisoner. The priest spoke of 'treason and rebellion'.

   2 marks

Page 38

Here's Looking at Yew

1. You measure its circumference (how far it is around its trunk). Each foot is equal to thirty years. Girth means the distance around the tree trunk.

   2 marks

2. The timber is deep gold with a red core and is easy to carve.
   It has been used for: wheels, cogs, axles, spoons, bowls, spears, arrows, bows and ships' nails.
   It was picked because it is easy to carve and is both hard and springy.

   1 mark
   1 mark for at least 3 items
   2 marks for why

3. Yew nails were made in shipbuilding. They were chosen because they were very hard. The Vikings used yew nails.

   2 marks for all 3 points

4. In 1215 King John signed the Magna Carta. It is believed to have been signed under the Ankerwyke Yew in Wraysbury near Windsor.

   For 2 marks you must make it clear that the yew tree connection is not certain

5. No marks for being surprised or not. Marks are awarded for the reasoning. Acceptable answers would be:
   - Amazed (or not) that a yew spear could kill an elephant.
   - Amazed (or already knew) that elephants once lived in Germany.
   - Surprised (or not) that a wooden spear was preserved for 90,000 years.

   3 marks for 2 or more points

6. Longevity is used to describe the yew tree because many of the trees we see today are more than 1000 years old. That is old compared to other trees.

   2 marks

Page 40
Plurals

1 stripes 2 tomatoes 3 attempts 4 foxes 5 guesses 6 bees 7 wishes
8 keys 9 babies 10 butterflies 11 guides 12 techniques 13 places
14 thieves 15 dresses 16 werewolves 17 women 18 pennies
19 pianos 20 zoos

Page 41
Spelling rules

Verb	Past tense	Present tense	Future tense
To fill	I have filled, I filled, I was filling	I fill, I am filling	I will fill
To love	I have loved, I loved, I was loving	I love, I am loving	I will love
To please	I have pleased, I pleased, I was pleasing	I please, I am pleasing	I will please
To write	I have written, I wrote, I was writing	I write, I am writing	I will write
To knock	I have knocked, I knocked, I was knocking	I knock, I am knocking	I will knock
To wrap	I have wrapped, I wrapped, I was wrapping	I wrap, I am wrapping	I will wrap
To tunnel	I have tunnelled, I tunnelled, I was tunnelling	I tunnel, I am tunnelling	I will tunnel
To receive	I have received, I received, I was receiving	I receive, I am receiving	I will receive
To hear	I have heard, I heard, I was hearing	I hear, I am hearing	I will hear
To surprise	I have surprised, I surprised, I was surprising	I surprise, I am surprising	I will surprise
To attempt	I have attempted, I attempted, I was attempting	I attempt, I am attempting	I will attempt
To change	I have changed, I changed, I was changing	I change, I am changing	I will change
To choose	I have chosen, I chose, I was choosing	I choose, I am choosing	I will choose
To fight	I have fought, I fought, I was fighting	I fight, I am fighting	I will fight
To cough	I have coughed, I coughed, I was coughing	I cough, I am coughing	I will cough

Page 42-43
Common spelling errors

1 author 2 audience 3 rhythm 4 theatre 5 government
6 ocean 7 island 8 neighbour 9 village 10 circumference
11 perimeter 12 sphere 13 research 14 engine 15 choir
16 orchestra 17 exit 18 February 19 necessary 20 cemetery 21 luggage 22 cinema 23 excellent 24 deafening 25 library 26 wrapper

Page 44-45
Ellipsis

1 "If you don't get this bedroom tidy, I'm..." Dad's threat was cut short by an exasperated sigh.
2 "Six pounds fifty? With that I could have bought…" Mum shook her head for once lost for words.
3 "Enough is enough," Mr Cheng warned. "Next time I find you in my garden I'm going to..." His voice trailed away as he waved his finger menacingly in our direction.
4 "The things I could tell you about my days," Aunt Ida mused "Such parties..." Her eyes had a faraway look as her voice trailed off and she relived those distant days.
5 If the purse was in his bedroom it would be alright, but if not...

Page 46
Dash

1 "You can have 50p to get yourself some chocolate – though you'd be better off with an apple – but be sure to bring me the rest of the change," instructed Aunt Emma.
2 As she shook the clothes from the plastic bag – a thoroughly unpleasant job – the purse fell out and lay accusingly on top of the pile.
3 Tara pushed her way to the front of the line – as I knew she would – desperate to be first to tell.
4 Of all the piglets in the barn – and there were many – Noah was the only one to allow himself to be petted.

Page 47
Semi-colon

1 Harry had his hair cut extremely short; Tom changed his mind and just had a trim.
2 We all took off our shoes; Uncle Rufus was very fussy about dirt on his Turkish rugs.
3 Now both teams were down to ten men; our defeat was looking a little less certain!
4 His fears had been quite exaggerated; the driver barely glanced at his bus pass.
5 There wasn't a moment to lose; the tide was coming in rapidly.
6 The dentist's face came closer and closer; her sweaty hands gripped the arms of the chair.

Page 48
Writing lists
1. You will need: scissors, a glue stick, four matches, a washing-up bottle and a ball of string.
2. Pacific islands are sometimes divided according to the people who live there: Melanesia in the west; Micronesia in the north; and Polynesia in the east.
3. The time a planet takes to orbit the Sun depends on its position in the Solar System: Mercury, the nearest planet, takes 88 days; Earth takes 365.256 days; Pluto, the most distant planet, takes nearly 250 years.
4. Some of the more common rock types are: sedimentary rocks such as coal and chalk; metamorphic rocks such as marble and quartzite; and igneous rocks such as granite and basalt.
5. Eating insufficient vitamins can cause many illnesses: loss of energy, bleeding gums, teeth falling out, bent bones, bad breath and blood problems.

Page 49
Punctuation passage
The night was still and silent. I started to run. "I MUST be getting closer to the shed," I muttered to myself, but however much I ran it seemed just as far away. Running faster now, I tripped on the uneven path and skidded along the gravel on my knees. I began crying, as much from fear as from the pain in my legs. I tried to get up but couldn't; the pain in my leg was too great. Was my leg broken?

In the dark night, and with my tearful eyes, I couldn't see clearly but I could feel the presence of someone close beside me. So much had already happened to me that night that suddenly I didn't feel afraid - it was more a sense of intrigue. Was there really a person near me that I couldn't see or was it something more? I reached out cautiously, trying to feel for something that I recognised. At first there was nothing, then suddenly a warm, fluffy material. "What's that? Who are you?" I whispered urgently.

"Matthew... Matt..." the voice responded. "It's time for bed. What are you doing out here?"

NOTE
Because punctuation is about putting your voice in the writing, you may have slightly different punctuation in parts of this passage, for example "Matthew? Matt?" the voice responded. would also be correct. However, in the main your punctuation should mirror the answer passage.

Page 50-51
Simile
Here are some suggested simile answers. Compare them with yours and decide which you prefer. How could you use them?
1. Silence – as if a wicked fairy had cast her spell and everything slept
2. Temper – like a storm cloud always threatening to break
3. A hat – like a giant fruit bowl
4. Arguing – words shot like arrows
5. A mouth – lips closed tight like a mussel
6. Running – as if chased by a pack of hungry wolves

Personification
Suggested answers.
The rain fought; The house welcomed; The flowers smiled; The sofa hugged; The book beckoned; The car screamed

Page 52-53
Nouns and verbs
Suggested answers
1. Dad stuffed The Times into his briefcase and dashed off to work.
2. Mr Patel smiled as I studied the giant size Galaxy bar. "You're still a chocoholic, I see," he teased.
3. Perched on the back seat of the Number 36 was a border collie, looking – it must be said – quite untroubled!
4. Slinging a raincoat over her shoulders, she strode off into the storm.

Adjectives
Suggested answers.
Joyous, celebrating, cheering crowd
Sullen, mocking, unmoving crowd
Reassuring, ecstatic, enthusiastic teacher
Stern, glowering, threatening teacher
Gentle, swaying, protective trees
Cruel, dense, unyielding trees
Calm, starry, peaceful night
Lonely, stormy, wild night

Adverbs
Suggested answers.

Whispered excitedly	Whispered hoarsely
Ran carelessly	Ran cautiously
Laughed quietly	Laughed as if his sides would split
Knocked desperately	Knocked lightly
Danced joyfully	Danced reluctantly
Slept peacefully	Slept fitfully

Alliteration
Suggested answers.
Swans gliding gracefully on the lake.
He watched wearily as the children filed out.
Dancing daintily from flower to flower, the fairy queen collected nectar.
The giant towered terrifyingly over us.

Here is an example using a familiar nursery rhyme to illustrate the point:

Little Miss Muffet,
Sat on a tuffet,
Eating her curds and whey,
There came a big spider,
Who sat down beside her,
And frightened Miss Muffet away.

1 Deduce

Question How old do you think Little Miss Muffet is?

Answer A child, probably under ten because she is called Little Miss. She sits on a tuffet, however she is not a toddler as she is able to eat by herself.

2
2 marks
1a

2 Infer

Question What would Little Miss Muffet do if she saw a minibeast running up her bedroom wall?

Answer She might scream, call out or run away because she is scared of small creatures/minibeasts.

2
2 marks
2a

3 Evaluate

Question Why do you think little children like this rhyme?

Answer Many children are scared of spiders and can relate to Little Miss Muffet. It has short lines, a simple rhyming pattern and rhythm, which makes it easy for young children to learn. When Miss Muffet is frightened away, young children have a chance to feel braver than she was.

3
3 marks
3a

4 Justify

Question Arachnophobia means to be afraid of spiders. Is it true to say Little Miss Muffet was arachnophobic? Use the text to answer the question.

Answer Little Miss Muffet was afraid of spiders because the rhyme says "and frightened Miss Muffet away".

2
2 marks
4a

Chicken Dinner

The following comprehension exercises give you practice in answering 2 and 3 mark questions. Beside each question are shown the marks your answer could earn. Reading between the lines will enable you to achieve Level 5!

When you have finished, go to the answer section of this book where appropriate answers are given.

Chicken Dinner

By Valerie Bloom

Mama, don' do it, please
Don' cook that chicken fe dinner,
We know that chicken from she hatch
She is the only one in the batch
That the mangoose didn't catch,
Please don' cook her fe dinner.

Mama, don' do it, please,
Don' cook that chicken fe dinner,
Yuh mean to tell me yuh feget
Yuh promise her to we as a pet?
She not even have a chance fe lay yet
And yuh want fe cook her fe dinner.

Mama don' do it, please,
Don' cook that chicken fe dinner,
Don't give Henrietta the chop,
I tell yuh what, we could swap
We will get yuh one from the shop
If yuh promise not to cook her fe dinner.

Mama, me really glad yuh know
That yuh never cook Henny fe dinner,
And she really glad too, I bet,
Oh Lawd, me suddenly feel upset.
Yuh don' suppose is somebody else pet
We eating now fe dinner?

Glossary

don' = don't   fe = for   yuh = you

Use the poem to answer these questions.

1 Give two reasons why the writer doesn't want the chicken cooked for dinner. Why do you think the writer is so attached to the chicken?

It is because the writer might of know it since it hatched, it's the only one left in the batch that didn't get taken by the mongoose and the mother promised her that she was going to be their pet.

2 Where do you think this poem is set? Give reasons for your answer.

I think it's set in a farm yard or a field because those are the places were most chickens (alive) live and it says we know that chicken from she hatched and she's the only one in the batch maybe she's the only one left in the place were they keep chickens.

3 What clues are there in this poem about the age of the chicken? How does the child use this as an argument for keeping the chicken longer?

In the poem it said that she not even have a chance fe lay yet which mean she isn't an adult she hasn't pruducduced and he's saying like she hasn't lived long are you already want to kill her!

4 What impact does using Henrietta's name have on Mama?

The child is trying to persuade her not to cook Henrietta for dinner and has given her an alternative so she changes her mind.

5 What horrible truth does the writer realise at the end of the poem, and how does that make him/her feel? might

He's realised that it of been someone else's pet that they were going to eat for dinner, that's it's better not to kill a young chicken and he's glad that they didn't cook Henny for dinner.

Fair's Fair

There was a candle burning on a table in the hall and a smell of onions, gravy and roast beef.

"Anybody home?" called Jackson, up a grand staircase that lost itself in shadows.

"Home" came down an echo "Home – home – home!"

"I brung back your dog!"

"Dog – dog – dog!"

"I've got to be going now!"

"Now – now – now!"

"Well," said Jackson. "Somebody must be about. Somebody must have lit the candle. Maybe they've fallen asleep."

He began to look, first in one room, then in another, then in another. They were all dark and nobody answered when he called. He went upstairs, and the dog followed after, growling and whining all the way. There was a glimmer of light coming from under a door. Jackson knocked. No answer. He called. No answer. He turned the handle and went inside.

What a room! As long as a street, nearly, and tall and wide to match! Candles in silver candlesticks, pictures in gold frames, china plates on a shining table, roast beef on a sideboard and a roaring fire in the grate! What a room! And there in a chair big enough for six, at the head of the table, with knife, fork and munching mouth, sat a small, thin, dirty, tattered, angry little girl!

"I brung back your dog," said Jackson, "miss."

She finished up what she was eating and put down her knife and fork.

"Not my dog," said she. "Too big, too black and too hungry for me."

"He had your key," said Jackson, eyeing the roast beef and watching the gravy. "Under his collar, miss."

"Not my key," said she. "Key of the house, that's all."

"Not your house then? How did you come here?"

"How did you come here?" Jackson told her.

"Same like me," she said. "Day before yesterday, just after dark."

"And you're still here?"

1 Why do you think the author describes the smell in the house?

So the description tells us what it the house smell of and that someone might be living their.

1 / 2 marks

2 Use three of your own adjectives, or adjectival phrases, to describe the house that Jackson enters.

As Jackson approched the semi-detached house, the vase house or the shadowy or the echoy.

2 / 2 marks

3 What does the echo tell the reader about the house and how is personification used to develop this idea?

That the house is echoy and he put it to the limit because he wrote ... home - home - home!

0 / 2 marks

4 What do these descriptions lead the reader to believe about the house?

It's like to build up the tension and make the readers think it's deserted.

2 / 2 marks

5 a) Why does the writer use short sentences?

To get the reader intersted and to make an effect.

b) In your opinion does this work? (refer to the text)

It does work because your eger to know what's going to happen (to build tension).

6 What does the description of the room tell us about the owner of the house?

That they were rich and posh because they had candels in silver candelsticks, pictures in gold frames and china plates.

7 Why might the little girl be angry?

She might be angry because he interpted her when she was eating and that nobody else is in the house

8 What can you infer about the little girl's personality by the way she responds to Jackson's arrival? Use examples from the text to support your answer.

She's got attiude, knows what she's doing (confident) and she's full of her self.

9 Find three examples of colloquial speech in this extract. Why is colloquial speech used?

'I brung your dog' 'not my dog too big too black and too hungry for me' 'He had your key' 'not my key, house key' 'not your house ?...' 'same like you' to start a intence atmosphere.

10 Why do Jackson and the little girl speak to each other in short sentences during this exchange? What does this tell us about their characters?

They are getting straight to the ponit not wasting time and Jackson is kind and friendly and the girl is confident.

Total marks: 12/20

Applemoon

Something woke me: startle-sound
or moonlight. The house dreamt
like an old cat, but I
looked out my window.

And night was day in a midnight
moon-flood. Mazy moon
flaring a halo of quick clouds
running the big black sky.
And I saw a thousand windfall apples
lying luminous as sea-stone beached
below the spiky silver trees.

So, shivering I
mouse-went out
with a basket, barefoot, toes
curling in the cold;
and singing soft
took ripe reluctant apples
under close and curious stars.

Only soon I saw
my shadow was not
the same as I;
it stooped more-
had its own thinness...
and our fingers
never met.

I quick-ran back
the house so
sleepy-warm, sure.
But looking out through curtain lace
I saw my shadow linger
moving slow and crooked, plucking
shadow apples
from the shining moony grass.

By Rose Flint

1 What does 'The house dreamt like an old cat' mean?
How does this contrast with the poet's feelings?

2 marks

2 Describe what the poet could see from her window.

2 marks

3 a) Find three examples of alliteration in the poem.

_____
_____

3a 1 mark

b) Why do you think the poet used alliteration here?

_____
_____
_____

3b 3 marks

4 What has happened to the poet's shadow and why?

_____
_____
_____
_____

4 3 marks

5 a) Find three examples where the poet links words with a hyphen.

_____
_____

5a 1 mark

b) Why do you think she does this?

_____
_____
_____
_____

5b 2 marks

6 Do you like the poem? Give your reasons.

_____
_____
_____
_____
_____

6 2 marks

Total marks

Fire, Bed and Bone

Chapter 5

We were not, nor would ever be, truly wild. I had known fireside, bed and bone, Rufus's pat and his soft look. All of my life up till then had been lived in the village. But still I was no hand-fed house dog. I knew what to do and how to do it. And the summer had started which brings easy living.

I carried Fleabane, curled limp from my jaws, bouncing and swinging up the hill above the village. Halfway to the top there was a pile of rocks that jutted out from under an earth mound. It smelled a bit of fox, but there were none there at the time. I crept in underneath the rocks, with Fleabane still held safely in my jaws. A passage led back right inside the mound. There was more rock in there and dry, white bones and a spear and helmet with the skull still inside it, all so old that not the faintest whiff of people hung about them.

There was a little pile of soft ash near the helmet. Something had burned there, long ago. It made a smooth bed for my Fleabane, and I laid him down. He wanted me to stay with him, but I was hungry.

There was a rabbit warren down at the bottom of the hill, on Great House land. Dawn was coming, when the rabbits would come out to crop and nibble.

I caught one, snapped its neck and felt its warm flesh and blood bringing me life and strength. I caught another one and carried it back to my new home. I let Fleabane nose its fur, though he was too young to eat it.

When I had fed and washed Fleabane, I left him sleeping and went to lie in the mouth of our den. It was a strange and lonely feeling, watching the sun come up, hearing the birds wake and seeing cows at pasture below.

Towards midday I saw what I'd been watching for. A group of soldiers, with four prisoners between them. Rufus and Comfort and two neighbours. Ede was not with them. Wat and Will and Alice might still be safe with her.

I woke Fleabane and told him I must go away but not for long, and that he must stay in the lair and not for any reason put his small brown nose outside it. There was still one rabbit leg for him to play with.

I wanted to run straight to Rufus, to hear his voice, to feel his hand on my head, to lick Comfort's brown hand. But I feared the soldiers. So I sneaked along, belly to the ground, dodging behind bushes, keeping low in ditches. Rufus did not see me. If he had seen me and called I would have run to him.

The soldiers took him to the stables in the yard of the Great House and pushed him and Comfort and the other two, all four into one stall. They shut and locked the doors behind them. One soldier stood outside.

The priest came and gabbled some rigmarole outside the stable door. I doubt if they could hear him inside. He spoke of treason and rebellion and King Richard's men. He spoke of law courts and execution. Beton, the miller's wife, watched with tears running down her face.

There is an old dog, Filbert, in the Great House yard, and I knew that he would watch the stable and bring me news so I went back to Fleabane.

On the way I saw Humble, hunting along the edge of the village. She spat at me. She has no loyalty at all.

1 What is the narrator of this story and how do you know? [3 marks]

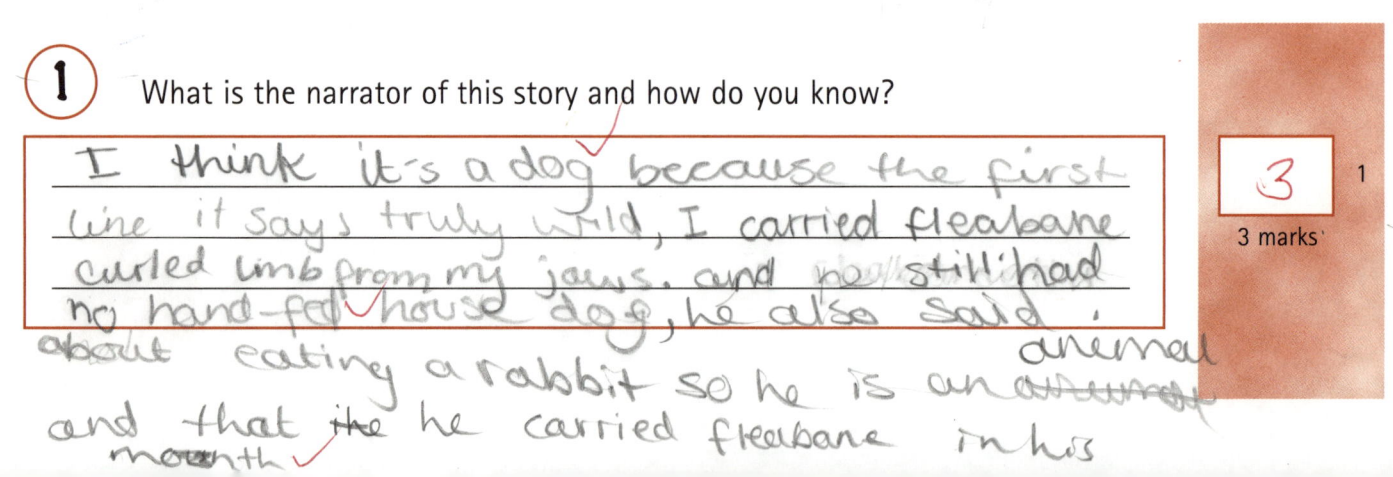

2 What does the writing tell you about the person who hid in the passage behind the rocks?

That they were quiet slim because they had fit behind the rocks and he also was carring fleabane so he was quiet strong and they were hiding from the soilders.

0 / 2 marks

3 Why do you think the person was hiding? Find two pieces of evidence to support your idea.

I think because: he was in danger and he was scared because it said "But I feard the soilders" and maybee he was scared that the soilder would take him prisoner too.

1 / 2 marks

4 a) What is Fleabane? How old is he?

Fleabane is a dog and he's a puppy because it said he was too young to eat a rabbit.

1 / 1 mark

b) Give two reasons for your answer.

He's a dog because: he need to be carried by the mounth of someone (dog) he's young because he was too young to eat rabbit. because he's a puppy.

1 / 2 marks

5 a) What is the relationship between the storyteller and Rufus and Comfort?

The relationship between them is very good because the storyteller wanted to run to Rufus and it wanted to like Comfort.

1 / 1 mark

b) Give two adjectives you would use to describe the relationship.

Fantastic and they are kind to one and another.

1 / 2 marks

6 What happened to Rufus and Comfort? What reason did the priest give for this?

The soilders took them to a stable locked up in one stall and the priest he spoke of treason and rebellion and law court and exucution.

2 / 2 marks

Total marks: 10 / 13

Here's Looking at Yew

The yew has survived the great climatic changes of our planet – fossils date back more than 140m years. Many yews we see today are more than 1,000 years old. Its longevity attracts more folklore than any other tree.

The age of a yew can be determined by its trunk – its girth increases by a foot every 30 years. A yew whose trunk measures 25 feet will have stood since the first millennium.

There are seven species of yew. Taxus baccata is native to the UK and grows best on limestone and chalk soils. The beautiful dense, deep golden timber with its red core is easy to carve and was used to make wheels, cogs, axles, spoons, bowls and even the body of the lute.

The Vikings trusted hard-as-iron yew nails to hold ships together, and yew weapons can be found in museums across the country. The oldest wooden artifact found was a spear made of yew, 150,000 years old and buried in peat in Essex. A 90,000-year-old yew spear was found preserved in peat between an elephant's ribs in Germany. But it was the yew's unique combination of hard heart and springy outer wood that armed English archers with the famous longbow.

The Yew in History

- Three English kings died from arrows fired from yew bows: Harold, Rufus and Richard 1.
- The Magna Carta is believed to have been signed by King John under the Ankerwyke Yew in the village of Wraysbury, near Windsor, in 1215.
- The Fortingall Yew in Perthshire is up to 5,000 years old and reputedly marks the birthplace of Pontius Pilate, whose father was stationed there.

READING COMPREHENSION 39

1 Explain how you work out the age of a yew tree. What does the word 'girth' mean?

2 marks

2 Describe the yew timber. What has it been used for and why was it picked over other timbers?

4 marks

3 In times past yew trees were used in shipbuilding. Which parts of the ship were made from yew? Why was yew chosen for this function?
Which invading civilisation used these ships?

2 marks

4 When was the Magna Carta signed and by whom? What connection does this event have with a yew tree?

2 marks

5 In the extract it says 'A 90,000-year-old yew spear was found preserved in peat between an elephant's ribs in Germany'. Do you find this information surprising? Explain your answer.

3 marks

6 'Longevity' means long life. Find this word in the text. What is it used to describe and why is it used?

2 marks

Total marks

Spelling practice

The following sections cover words or rules where mistakes are commonly made. Check your answers at the end – are you consistently making mistakes in one area? Check the appropriate spelling rule again.

Plurals

Here is a list of words. You need to write them in the plural form.

1. stripe — Stripes
2. tomato — tomatos
3. attempt —
4. fox — foxes
5. guess — guesses
6. bee —
7. wish — wishes
8. key —
9. baby — babies
10. butterfly — butterflies
11. guide —
12. technique —
13. place —
14. thief —
15. dress —
16. werewolf —
17. woman — Womens
18. penny —
19. piano —
20. zoo — zoo's

Spelling rules

Fill in the following chart. By putting the different verbs into the past, present and future tenses you will be covering many of the spelling rules. If you are having difficulty spelling these words, you need to identify which spelling rule you are having trouble with. Revise it and have another go.

Verb	Past tense	Present tense	Future tense
To fill	I have filled, I filled, I was filling	I fill, I am filling	I will fill
To love	I have loved, I was loving, I loved	I love, I am loving	I will love
To please			
To write			
To knock			
To wrap			
To tunnel			
To receive			
To hear			
To surprise			
To attempt			
To change			
To choose			
To fight			
To cough			

Common spelling errors

- Read the following clues. Each has a one-word answer.
- Work out what the word is and then spell it.

When you have finished, check your spelling against the answers. How did you do?

1. Someone who writes books. — Is an author
2. People who listen to a performance — Are audience
3. The beat in a song. — Is a rythme
4. Where you go to enjoy a play. — You go to the playground
5. The political party that runs the country.
6. A body of water larger than the sea.
7. Land surrounded by water.
8. The person who lives next door. — Is a neighbour
9. Smaller than a town.
10. All the way around the outside of a circle.
11. All the way around the outside of a rectangle.
12. The mathematical name for a ball. — It a football

13. To investigate something. — A detecluve
14. Another name for a motor. —
15. A group who sing together. —
16. A large group who play instruments together. — Is a band
17. The way out. —
18. The second month. — Is February
19. It has to be done. —
20. Where dead people are buried. — In a graveyard
21. Cases and bags to take on holiday. —
22. A place you visit to watch a film. — Is a cenima
23. Extremely good. —
24. Incredibly loud. —
25. Where books are kept to be borrowed. —
26. What chocolate is contained in. — A factory.

Adding 'voice' to your writing

If you are aiming to achieve Level 5 you will already know the basics of sentence punctuation and be using capital letters, full stops, question marks, exclamation marks and commas accurately. In this section you will practise the more advanced punctuation you will need to use to achieve Level 5.

Ellipsis

Example
"He said if I didn't give it to him he'd tell Mr McDonald that I cheated in the last test," Theo said fearfully.

Using an ellipsis (...) to hint at the bullying is much more powerful.
"He said if I didn't give it to him he'd…" Theo's voice trailed away.

Re-write these sentences using an ellipsis.

1 "If you don't get this bedroom tidy, I'm stopping your pocket money for a month and you won't watch any television this weekend," Dad threatened with an exasperated sigh.

_____
_____
_____

2 "Six pounds fifty? With that I could have bought countless pens, pencils, rubbers and notebooks," Mum complained.

_____
_____
_____

3 "Enough is enough," Mr Cheng warned. "Next time I find you in my garden I'm going to phone the police and then you might learn to respect other people's property," he said waving his finger menacingly in our direction.

_____
_____
_____

PUNCTUATION   45

4 "The things I could tell you about my days," Aunt Ida mused. "Such parties, the ball gowns, men in dinner suits, an orchestra playing a waltz while young men queued up to ask me to dance. Oh yes those were the days." Aunt Ida's eyes had a faraway look as in her mind she relived those distant days.

5 If the purse was in his bedroom it would be alright, but if not he was in real trouble and that didn't bear thinking about.

WARNING

Do not overuse ellipsis – one or two uses in a story is enough.
Too many will spoil the effect.

Write some more speech sentences with ellipsis in your own notebook.
Use the following phrases that describe why the speech has stopped.

- leaving the question unanswered
- his voice trailed away
- the words were cut short by a scream
- his voice disappeared into a whisper
- laughter drowning the rest of her tale

Dash

A dash (–) is used in informal writing to add asides or afterthoughts.

Examples
After we'd climbed to the top of the hill – the highest one in the county – we stopped for a well earned rest.

Dad nodded seriously as Mr Thomas reeled off the list of unfinished homework, detentions and other misdemeanours – he'd kept a very detailed list!

Insert the following asides or afterthoughts into the sentences below using dashes to punctuate them. They are numbered to help you.

1. though you'd be better off with an apple
2. a thoroughly unpleasant job
3. as I knew she would
4. and there were many

1 "You can have 50p to get yourself some chocolate but be sure to bring me the rest of the change," instructed Aunt Emma.

2 As she shook the clothes from the plastic bag the purse fell out and lay accusingly on top of the pile.

3 Tara pushed her way to the front of the line desperate to be first to tell.

4 Of all the piglets in the barn Noah was the only one to allow himself to be petted.

Semi-colon

Semi-colons can be used in place of a connective to join two closely-related clauses. This forces the reader to make the link between the ideas.

Replace the connective in these sentences with a semicolon.
Read both sentences and decide which you prefer.

1 Harry had his hair cut extremely short however Tom changed his mind and just had a trim.

2 We all took off our shoes because Uncle Rufus was very fussy about dirt on his Turkish rugs.

3 Now both teams were down to ten men and our defeat was looking a little less certain!

4 His fears had been quite exaggerated as the driver barely glanced at his bus pass.

5 There wasn't a moment to lose as the tide was coming in rapidly.

6 The dentist's face came closer and closer as her sweaty hands gripped the arms of the chair.

Writing lists

To achieve Level 5, you must use colons, semi-colons and commas correctly in a list.

The rules are:
- use a colon to introduce a list
- use commas to separate single items in a list
- use semi-colons to separate phrases or clauses in a list

Punctuate these lists.

1 You will need scissors a glue stick four matches a washing-up bottle and a ball of string.

2 Pacific islands are sometimes divided according to the people who live there Melanesia in the west Micronesia in the north and Polynesia in the east.

3 The time a planet takes to orbit the Sun depends on its position in the Solar System Mercury the nearest planet takes 88 days Earth takes 365.256 days Pluto the most distant planet takes nearly 250 years.

4 Some of the more common rock types are sedimentary rocks such as coal and chalk metamorphic rocks such as marble and quartzite and igneous rocks such as granite and basalt.

5 Eating insufficient vitamins can cause many illnesses loss of energy bleeding gums teeth falling out bent bones bad breath and blood problems.

Test your punctuation

This passage has been written without any punctuation. Rewrite it with the correct punctuation.

the night was still and silent I started to run I must be getting closer to the shed I muttered to myself but however much I ran it seemed just as far away running faster now I tripped on the uneven path and skidded along the gravel on my knees I began crying as much from fear as from the pain in my legs I tried to get up but couldn't the pain in my leg was too great was my leg broken in the dark night and with my tearful eyes I couldnt see clearly but I could feel the presence of someone close beside me so much had already happened to me that night that suddenly I didnt feel afraid it was more a sense of intrigue was there really a person near me that I couldnt see or was it something more I reached out cautiously trying to feel for something that I recognised at first there was nothing then suddenly a warm fluffy material whats that who are you I whispered urgently matthew matt the voice responded it's time for bed what are you doing out here

Every word counts

Level 5 writers choose every word with care and variety is the secret.

Simile

A simile creates a sharp description using very few words by making a comparison with something else, often using *like* or *as*.

Example

Heat – like a devil's furnace

Write your own similes to describe the following.

1. Silence	4. Arguing
2. Temper	5. A mouth
3. A hat	6. Running

Metaphor

Creates a description by saying something is something else. It is a very powerful descriptive device. Some metaphors give objects human attributes – this is called personification.

Write your own sentences containing these metaphors.

① the knife of fear

② big spaniel eyes

③ a graveyard silence

VOCABULARY 51

4 the fog was a blanket

5 the sun smiled its welcome

6 darkness ready to pounce

Personification

Personification is when we give human characteristics to a non-human thing.

Example

The sun smiled down on the trees standing to attention.

Describe these nouns using personification.

The rain	The house
The flowers	The sofa
The book	The car

BEWARE

Do not overuse these techniques. One or two in each piece of writing is sufficient.

VOCABULARY

Nouns and verbs

Accurate nouns and powerful verbs can be more effective than adjectives and adverbs in some cases.

Rewrite these sentences improving the verbs and nouns.

1 Dad put the newspaper into his bag then went off to work.

___

2 The shopkeeper smiled as I looked at the biggest chocolate bar. "You're still a chocoholic, I see," he said.

___

3 Sitting on the back seat of the bus was a large, black and white dog, looking – it must be said – quite happy!

___

4 Putting on her coat, she went out into the cold and windy evening.

___

Adjectives

Adjectives are used to add something NEW to a noun e.g. *a severe look* is quite different from *an encouraging look*.

Add an adjective to the words in the first column to create a happy mood and in the second column to create a menacing mood.

	crowd		crowd
	teacher		teacher
	trees		trees
	night		night

Adverbs

Adverbs refine the meaning of a verb. Sometimes a phrase acts as an adverb e.g. sobbed *as if her heart would break*. Never use adverbs that mean the same as the verb, e.g. raced quickly.

Use an adverb to say something different about the verb in each column.

Whispered	Whispered
Ran	Ran
Laughed	Laughed
Knocked	Knocked
Danced	Danced
Slept	Slept

Alliteration

Choose words for their sound as well as their meaning. Words with the same initial sound work well together.

Add an alliterative adverb to these sentences.

Swans gliding _____ on the lake.

He watched _____ as the children filed out.

Dancing _____ from flower to flower, the fairy queen collected nectar.

The giant towered _____ over us.

Reviewing your work

Checking – or reviewing – your work is an important part of being a writer. No writer finishes without re-reading what has been written. There are always changes to be made – some are small and some are more significant. Without re-reading your work, you could easily miss the opportunity to make some important alterations and improvements.

So, when you are reviewing your work, what should you be looking for?

★ **Check that the main message of your writing has come through to the reader.** For example, if you are writing a suspense story, make sure that there is a feeling of anticipation and dread. If you are writing a persuasive piece, ask yourself, "Would I be persuaded to change my mind, or at least reconsider my position, after reading this?" If not, perhaps you need to look again at the guidelines for persuasive writing.

★ **Make sure you have followed the guidelines for the text type you have used.** It's very easy to slip into informal writing when you should be using something more formal. Reviewing helps you to pick up on those kinds of errors, which bring the standard of your writing down. If you are not sure if you have used the right language features or organisation, CHECK. Don't get worried about mistakes – just sort them out, and remember to correct that mistake in the future. REMEMBER, no-one gets it right all the time, but you can choose to learn from your mistakes.

★ **Check for basic spelling and grammar mistakes.** The easiest way to check for spelling is to re-read your work, looking carefully as you read. If you come to a word that just doesn't look right, trust your instincts – it probably needs another attempt! Write out a few options on a piece of paper. Do any of them look right? Then, if you can, get a dictionary and check. Try to learn the correct spelling once you have looked it up. You won't always have the option of looking it up! As you check for basic grammar mistakes, the easiest way is to read your work out loud. If you listen carefully to what you are reading, you should be able to 'hear' sections or sentences that don't sound quite right. Try re-writing your sentence in several combinations, and read them out loud. Which one sounds right? Trust your instinct. Good writers are not scared of words!

★ **Read as much as you can.** Read different types of books because it will help you to become accustomed to good writing. Then when you are checking your work, you will have a larger pool of ideas and phrases to draw on.

★ **Always write down other writer's good ideas, sentences, phrases or words.** There's nothing wrong with using parts of someone else's ideas. Remember, there's nothing new under the sun. If you like the phrase or you think it might be useful, jot it down in your writer's notebooks. You just never know when it could come in handy!

Handwriting

Your handwriting will be assessed through your two Writing tests. Below are examples of work awarded 1, 2 or 3 marks (out of 3). Have a good look at them and try to write in your best handwriting every time you do an activity from this book. How would you do? Try with different pencils and pens so that you are sure which tool gives you the best result. Remember, any crossings out may lose you marks, so rub out if you need to using a clean rubber.

Writing awarded 1 mark has letters that are always accurately formed and are consistent in size. It is partly joined or printed, and the letters and words are suitably spaced.

The writing below has been given 1 mark.

> *Henry shuffled slowly over to his mother, "Mum, I have to go and join the Light Brigade," he whispered.*

Writing awarded 2 marks is legible and joined, with the correct joins between letters. The ascenders (tall parts of the letter above the line) and descenders (tall parts of the letter below the line) are in proportion and parallel. Spacing between the words and letters is consistent.

The writing below has been given 2 marks.

> *Henry shuffled slowly over to his mother, "Mum I have to go and join the Light Brigade" he whispered*

Writing awarded 3 marks is controlled, confident and stylish, with consistency in joins, size and spacing all the way through. There are no crossings out and no obvious pauses in the writing. There are also no copying errors – if you get 3 marks, you will have taken care to get it exactly right.

The writing below has been given 3 marks.

> *Henry shuffled slowly over to his mother, "Mum, I have to go and join the Light Brigade," he whispered.*

Notes